The Greenwich Guide to

Measuring

Time

Heinemann Library
Chicago, Illinois

Graham Dolan

Royal Observatory Greenwich

Published by Heinemann Library,
an imprint of Reed Educational & Professional Publishing,
Chicago, IL
Customer Service 888-454-2279

Visit our website at www.heinemannlibrary.com

Designed by Celia Floyd
Illustrations by Jeff Edwards
Originated by Dot Gradations
Printed in Hong Kong/China

05 04 03 02 01
10 9 8 7 6 5 4 3 2 1

Library of Congress Cataloging-in-Publication Data
Dolan, Graham, 1953-
  Measuring time / Graham Dolan.
       p. cm. -- (The greenwich guide to)
Includes bibliographical references and index.
  ISBN 1-58810-043-X
  1. Time measurements--Juvenile literature. 2. Clocks and
watches--Juvenile literature. [1. Time measurements. 2. Clocks and
watches. 3. Time.] I. Title.
  QB213 .D48 2001
  528'.7--dc21

                                        00-010541

Acknowledgments
The publisher would like to thank the following for permission to reproduce photographs: National Maritime Museum, pp. 4, 5, 8, 9, 16 top and bottom, 17, 19 top and bottom, 20, 21 top and bottom, 22, 24, 25 top and bottom, 26, 27, 28, 29; Francisco Diego, pp. 7 both, 10; Ancient Art and Architecture, pp. 11, 12, 13; Science Photo Library, pp. 14, 15.

Cover photograph reproduced with permission of Telegraph Colour Library.

Spine logo reproduced with permission of the National Maritime Museum.

Every effort has been made to contact copyright holders of any material reproduced in this book. Any omissions will be rectified in subsequent printings if notice is given to the Publisher.

Some words are shown in bold, **like this.** You can find out what they mean by looking in the glossary.

Contents

What Is Time?

Everyone uses time. We can waste it. We can measure it. But we cannot see it or hear it. What is it? Why does it go forward but never backward?

People have asked these questions for thousands of **years.** Although no one has all the answers, scientists are able to measure time more **accurately** than ever before.

Clocks and calendars

We use **clocks** and **watches** to show us the time—the **hours,** the **minutes,** and the **seconds.** We use **calendars** to show us the date—the **day,** the **month,** and the year.

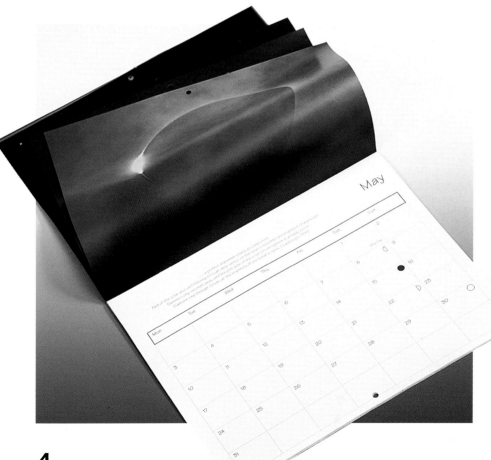

We use calendars to help us plan our lives.

4

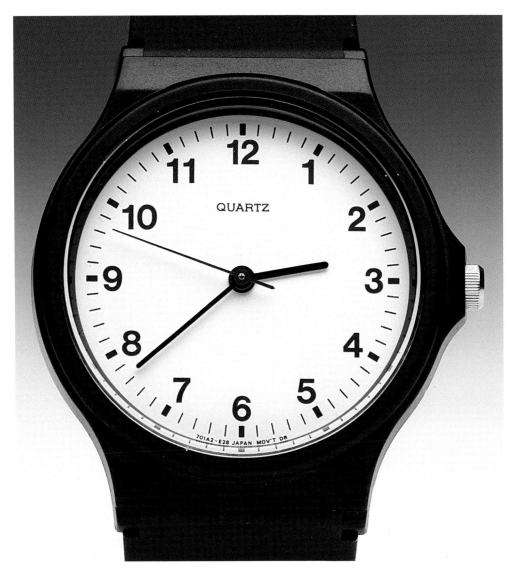

Clocks and watches show the time in hours, minutes, and seconds.

More and more accurate clocks

Four hundred years ago, the best clocks would lose or gain about fifteen minutes a day. Your watch is probably about 1,000 times more accurate than that. Today's watches lose or gain no more than a second a day. Although this sounds impressive, it is about five billion times less accurate than the world's most accurate clocks. These will lose or gain no more than a second in fifteen million years.

Patterns in Time

Days

Earth is spinning on its **axis.** As it spins around, we get darkness, then daylight, then darkness again. The pattern of daylight and darkness repeats itself each time Earth completes one full turn on its axis. This is because different parts of Earth are facing the Sun at different times. Our **day** is based on this repeating pattern.

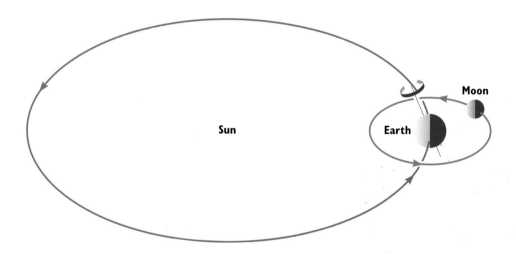

The length of our days, months, and years are linked to the movements of Earth and the Moon.

Months

The Moon **orbits** Earth. Its appearance in the sky changes in a pattern from one day to the next. The pattern repeats itself each time the Moon passes in its orbit between Earth and the Sun. Our **month** is based on this repeating pattern.

Years

Earth orbits the Sun. As it goes on its journey around the Sun, we pass from one season to the next. The pattern of the seasons repeats itself each time Earth starts a new orbit. Our **year** is based on this repeating pattern.

We get light and heat from the Sun. We also use the Sun to measure our days and years.

The appearance of the Moon changes as it orbits Earth. The picture on the right was taken three days after the one on the left.

Hours and Minutes

We divide our **day** into smaller parts called **hours.** In ancient times, the day was usually divided so that there were twelve hours of **daytime** and twelve hours of **nighttime.** However, daytime, or the time when the Sun is shining on our part of Earth, is longer in summer than in winter. In the summer, daytime hours lasted longer than nighttime ones. In the winter, nighttime hours lasted longer than daytime ones.

Today, we still divide our days into 24 hours. Now our hours are all the same length. Each hour is divided into 60 **minutes.** Each minute is divided into 60 **seconds.**

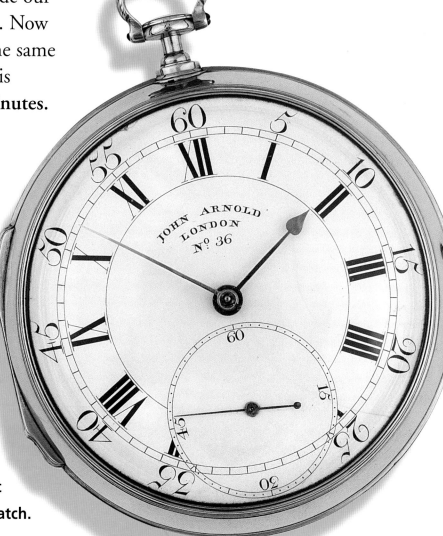

On most watches, the hour hand goes around twice each day. You can see that on this old pocket watch.

8

On a few **clocks** and watches, the hour
hand goes around once every 24 hours.

The decimal day

About 200 years ago, the French decided to change their
day. Each of their days was divided into ten hours. This
made each hour more than twice the length of a normal
hour. Each hour was divided into 100 minutes. Each
minute was divided into 100 seconds. Many people in
France and other countries did not like this decimal day.
In the end, the French stopped using it.

Calendars

Years

Our **year** is linked to the seasons. The pattern of the seasons repeats itself in just about $365\frac{1}{4}$ days. Because this is not a whole number of **days,** our **calendar** years have either 365 or 366 days. Years with 366 days are called **leap years.** They normally occur every four years. The extra day is added to the month of February.

Leap years

If the year number can be divided by four and does not end in 00, the year is a leap year. If it ends in 00, it is only a leap year if it can be divided by 400. So, the year 1900 was not a leap year, but 2000 was.

Months

Our **months** are linked to the movements of the Moon. The Moon passes between Earth and the Sun about every $29\frac{1}{2}$ days. When this happens, there is a new moon. In the Jewish and Muslim calendars, this marks a new month. All Jewish and Muslim months have either 29 or 30 days.

A new crescent moon appears at the start of each Jewish and Muslim month.

In the calendar we normally use, months are slightly longer. There are twelve of them in a year. Except for February, they have either 30 or 31 days. An old rhyme helps us remember how many days are in each month.

Thirty days hath September,
April, June, and November,
All the rest have thirty-one,
Excepting February alone,
Which hath but twenty-eight, in fine,
Till leap year gives it twenty-nine.

Many people today follow what is called a Gregorian calendar. It was named for Pope Gregory XIII, who based it on the Roman calendar introduced by Julius Caesar a little over 2,000 years ago. Some people use their own religious calendars as well. For instance, Muslim countries usually follow a calendar based on Islam rather than using the Gregorian calendar.

Julius Caesar created a system of leap years.

11

The Names of the Months

Our **calendar** was started by the Romans. At first, there were just ten named **months.** There was a break between December and March. This break had no name. It was later split into the months January and February.

January is named after the Roman god Janus. Janus had two faces. One looked forward to the future. One looked back to the past.

February is named after Februa, a Roman festival celebrated during that time.

Janus was the Roman god of doors, gates, and new beginnings.

March is named after Mars, the Roman god of war. In ancient Rome, March was the first month in the calendar.

April comes from the Latin word *aperire,* which means to open. In Rome, many flower buds started to open in April.

May is named after the Roman goddess of growth, Maia. Spring is a time of growth.

12

June may have been named after the Roman goddess of marriage, Juno. It may also have been named after a powerful family in ancient Rome—the Junius family.

July was originally called *Quintilis,* which means "the fifth month." After January and February were added, it became the seventh month of the year. Its name was changed to July, in honor of Julius Caesar.

August was originally called Sextilis. Sextilis means "the sixth month." It was renamed August to honor the Roman emperor Augustus.

September means "the seventh month." It is now the ninth month.

October means "the eighth month." It is now the tenth month.

November means "the ninth month." It is now the eleventh.

December means "the tenth month." It is now the twelfth.

Augustus was the first Roman emperor.

Day Names

In many European languages, the names of the **days** of the **week** come from the old Roman names. The Romans named the days of the week after the Sun, the Moon, and the planets Mars, Mercury, Jupiter, Venus, and Saturn. They believed that the Sun was a god, and named a day after him to keep him happy. Monday was named after the Moon. It was originally called the Moon's day. Saturday was named after the planet Saturn. We still use these Roman names for Sunday, Monday, and Saturday.

Saturn was the Roman god of farming. Both Saturday and the planet Saturn are named after him.

In France, the days are named after the Sun, the Moon, and the planets. Thursday, called *jeudi*, is named after the planet Jupiter, the largest planet in the solar system.

Our names for the other four days were later changed by the Anglo-Saxons. Tiu was their god of war and justice. Tuesday is named after him. Wednesday is named after the god Woden. Woden was Tiu's father, and he was the most powerful of the Anglo-Saxon gods. Thursday is named after the god Thor. Thor was the god of thunder. Friday is named after the goddess Frigg. Frigg was married to Woden, and was the goddess of marriage. She represented love and beauty.

Day Names	
Today	*In Saxon times*
Sunday	Sun's Day
Monday	Moon's Day
Tuesday	Tiu's Day
Wednesday	Woden's Day
Thursday	Thor's Day
Friday	Frigg's Day
Saturday	Saterne's Day

Timers

Timers are used to measure periods of time. We use them in the kitchen to make sure our food is properly cooked. Some cooks use a sand timer when boiling an egg. A sand timer that measures an hour is often called an hourglass.

To start a sand timer, you have to turn it upside down. The sand in this timer takes one minute to run back down to the bottom.

Unlike a clock, a kitchen timer is unable to tell you the time of day. It can measure only a short period of time. An alarm sounds when the set time has passed.

Pendulums

A swinging **pendulum** can also be used as a timer. You can make one from a weight and a length of thread. The longer your pendulum is, the longer it will take to swing from side to side.

From timer to clock

You can use a timer, such as a pendulum, to tell the time. Besides counting the swings, you would have to make sure it did not stop. You would also need to know exactly what time it was when you started counting.

Keeping track of the time is much easier with an automatic timer and counter. It is much less trouble to keep time with a normal **clock** or a **watch** than by counting the swings of a pendulum.

A pendulum that is 39 inches (99 centimeters) long will swing from side to side in about a **second**. To time a minute, you would have to count 60 swings of the pendulum.

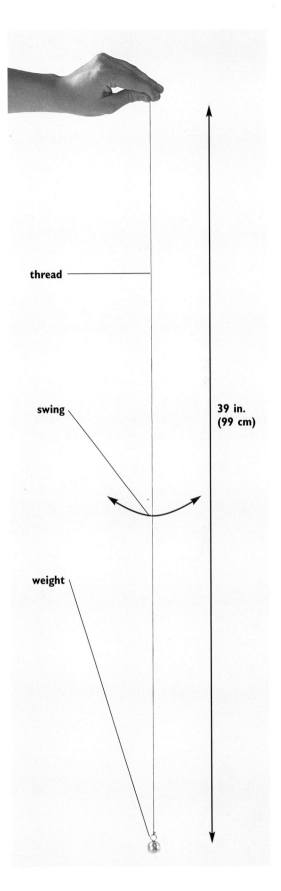

thread

swing

weight

39 in. (99 cm)

The First Clocks

From the earliest times, people used the movement of the Sun across the sky to tell the time. A **sundial** casts a shadow that uses the Sun's position to tell us the time.

The world's first mechanical **clocks** were made in Europe about 700 years ago. Most of them looked different from today's clocks. They told the time by ringing a bell, usually every **hour.** They were not very **accurate.** It was only later that hands were used. To start with, there was normally only an hour hand. It moved in the same direction that the Sun appears to move across the sky in the **Northern Hemisphere.** We call this direction **clockwise.**

Until about 350 years ago, the **timer** used in most clocks was a weighted metal crossbar that swung from side to side at a regular rate.

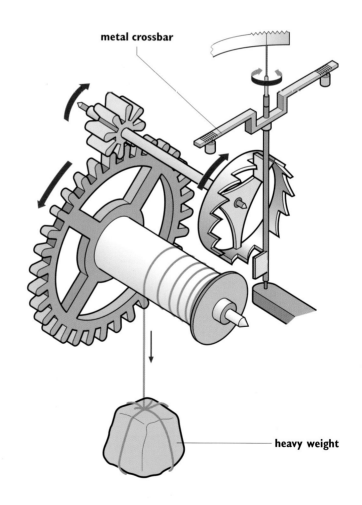

metal crossbar

heavy weight

18

In the **Southern Hemisphere,** the Sun always appears to move across the sky in the opposite direction. We call this direction **counterclockwise.** If clocks had been invented in Australia instead of in Europe, clockwise and counterclockwise might be the other way around!

This lantern clock was made in the 1600s. It started life with a weighted crossbar for a timer. Its timekeeping improved when this was changed to a **pendulum** in the 1800s. The pendulum swings from side to side twice each **second.**

pendulum

This **watch** is about 350 years old. Like the lantern clock, it has an hour hand, but no **minute** hand.

Today's Clocks and Watches

Pendulum clocks

Pendulums have been used as **timers** in **clocks** since 1656. They are still used in a few clocks today. Some clocks have long pendulums that swing from side to side once each **second.** Others have shorter pendulums that swing at a faster rate. The clock ticks each time the pendulum swings from side to side.

Inside the clock, there are lots of wheels with notches in them. Their job is to count the swings of the pendulum and make the hands move at the right rate.

pendulum

In this clock, the pendulum swings from side to side once every second.

Quartz clocks

The timer in almost all modern clocks and **watches** is a piece of **quartz** crystal. An electric current from the battery makes the crystal **vibrate** at a steady rate. In most quartz clocks and watches, it vibrates 32,768 times each second. An electronic circuit counts the vibrations. Every time 32,768 vibrations are counted, the second hand moves one step around the **dial**.

This is a quartz watch.

battery

The quartz timer is hidden from view inside this container.

Most of today's alarm clocks contain a quartz timer.

21

Astronomers and Timekeeping

We rely on scientists and **astronomers** to provide us with the exact time when we need it. They figure out the time by measuring how far Earth has turned on its **axis.** Until the 1970s, they did this using specially designed **telescopes** like the one shown below. The telescopes could point only in a north-south direction. They could be moved up and down, but not from side to side.

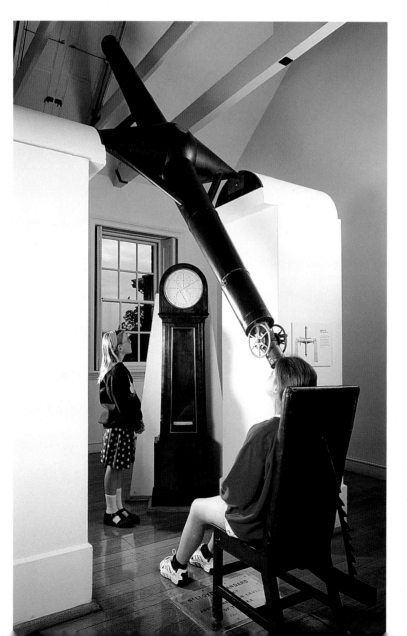

Until recently, most **observatories** had a telescope like this for finding the exact time. This one was used at the Royal Observatory in Greenwich, London, between 1816 and 1850.

Timekeeper Earth

As Earth turns on its axis, the stars seem to move across the sky. They appear to rise and set like the Sun. They are actually moving much more slowly. Every time Earth completes one full turn on its axis, the same stars reappear in front of the telescope.

Astronomers once used Earth, the stars, and the telescope like a **clock.** Earth was like the **timer,** spinning on its axis once each **day.** The telescope was like a clock hand, and the stars were like the numbers around the **dial.**

Today, astronomers measure how far Earth has turned by measuring the positions of **satellites.** The satellites are tracked using telescopes that can be turned to point anywhere in the sky.

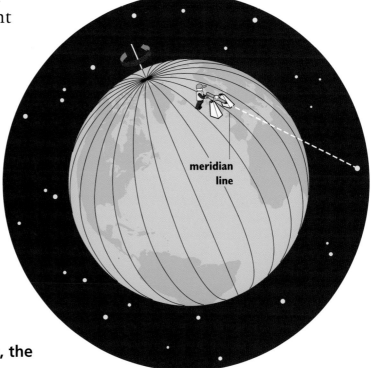

meridian line

We can use Earth, the stars, and a telescope to find the correct time.

What's the Time?

In the past, it was much more difficult than it is today to set a **clock** or **watch** to exactly the right time. Clocks were normally checked with a **sundial**. At best, sundials can be used to set a clock to about the nearest **minute**. People who needed to know the time more **accurately** had to use a special **telescope** or visit an **observatory**.

Between the 1830s and the 1930s, some clockmakers in London checked their clocks each week, using an accurate watch belonging to the Belville family. Ruth Belville is shown here checking her watch at the Royal Observatory in Greenwich, something she did each Monday morning.

Before watches became widely available, wealthy people would often use a portable sundial like this.

Time signals

Today, we can set our watches to the nearest fraction of a **second**. Many radio stations transmit a special time signal to tell people the exact time. The world's first radio time signals were transmitted by the U.S. Navy in 1904.

The first British time signals were transmitted by the BBC in 1924. They came from the Royal Observatory in Greenwich. They marked the **hours** of **Greenwich Mean Time.** Today, they normally consist of six tones, spaced one second apart. The last tone is longer than the rest and marks the start of a new hour.

The U.S. Naval Observatory in Washington, D.C., transmits similar time signals. They are used to set the standard time for the government.

This radio-controlled clock contains a radio receiver. It automatically adjusts itself to the correct time.

Atomic Clocks

More accurate than Earth

Atomic clocks are the most **accurate clocks** ever built. The first one was built about 50 years ago. They run at a steadier rate than Earth's rotation. Their incredible accuracy has led scientists to change the way in which they measure and describe the length of a **second**.

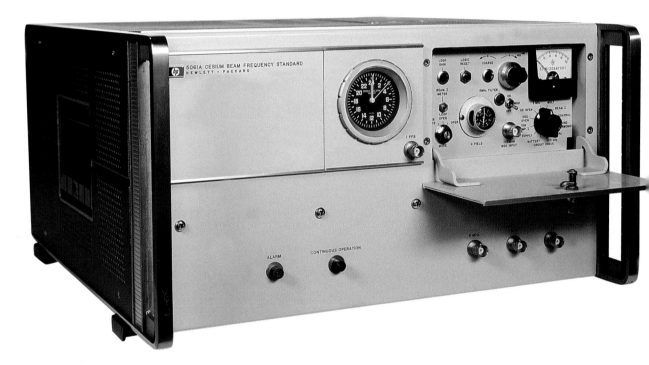

This cesium atomic clock will lose or gain no more than one second in 300,000 years.

The length of a second

A hundred **years** ago, a second was said to be 1/86,400 of an average **day**. Since 1967, scientists have described it as the time taken for 9,192,631,770 vibrations of the **timer** inside a cesium atomic clock to occur.

Leap seconds

Little by little, Earth is slowing down. Scientists use **satellites** and atomic clocks to measure how fast this is happening. In 1972, they decided to make some days one second longer than normal. They did this to keep Earth and the time shown by our clocks from getting out of step. The extra seconds they added are called **leap seconds.** One second has been added in most years since 1972. Radio-controlled clocks adjust themselves automatically when leap seconds are added.

Today's time signals are produced using atomic clocks. They give us accurate time. We do not each need to have an atomic clock of our own.

Mobile phone networks and satellite navigation systems need accurate timing methods. These systems would not work without atomic clocks.

Fact File

If Earth spun faster on its **axis,** our **days** would be shorter, and there would be more of them in a **year!**

Jupiter is the fastest-spinning planet and has the shortest days.

The **pendulum** in a grandfather **clock** swings from side to side 86,400 times a day. That is more than 31 million times a year!

The farther a planet is from the Sun, the longer it takes to complete one **orbit,** and the longer its year is. Earth is farther from the Sun than Mercury, so its years are longer.

Until 1676, nobody knew for certain that Earth spun on its axis at a steady rate. In that year, John Flamsteed discovered that it did. He made his discovery using clocks and a **telescope** at the Royal **Observatory** in Greenwich, London.

If Earth was as far away from the Sun as Pluto, it would complete less than half an orbit in your entire lifetime.

John Flamsteed was the first director of the Royal Observatory, Greenwich.

This was the first **watch** able to keep **accurate** time at sea. It allowed a sailor out of sight of land to calculate his position accurately. This had never been possible before. The watch was built by John Harrison and was tested at sea in 1762. His invention eventually won him a prize of £20,000. Winning that much money back then was about the same as it would be if you won the lottery today.

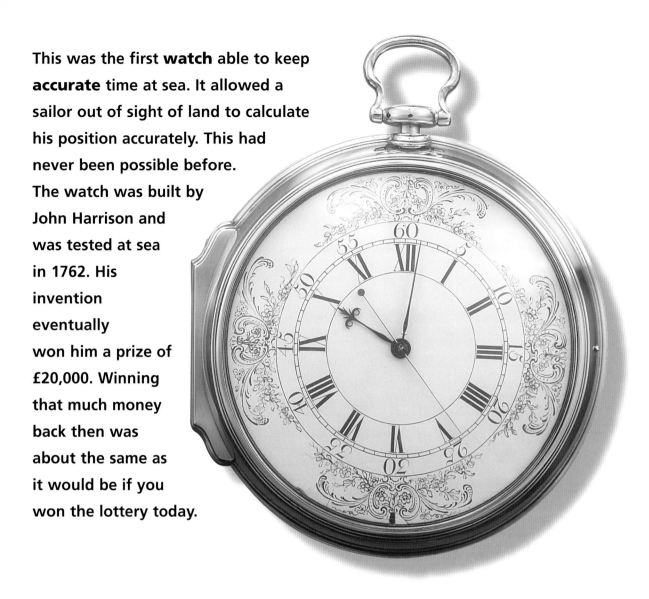

In the Muslim **calendar**, a year normally has 354 days.

In the Jewish calendar, some years have twelve **months.** Others have thirteen.

When the system of **leap years** first started, a mistake was made, and they were inserted every three years instead of every four.

A few weeks after your fifty-seventh birthday, you will have been alive for half a million **hours**!

29

Glossary

accurate   difference between the time shown and the actual time is very small

astronomer   someone who observes or studies the stars and planets

atomic clock   most accurate type of clock that has ever been built

axis   imaginary line passing through the center of a planet from the North to the South Pole, around which the planet spins

calendar   division of the year into days, weeks, and months

clock   device for measuring time

clockwise   direction in which the hands of a clock move

counterclockwise   opposite direction to the way in which the hands on a clock move

day   length of time based on the time it takes for Earth to spin around once on its axis

daytime   time between sunrise and sunset

dial   part of a clock or watch that shows the time

foliot   swinging bar used as a timer in the clocks made by the first clockmakers

Greenwich Mean Time   originally the accurate time, as calculated in the Royal Observatory Greenwich. It is used as a measure for calculating standard time.

hour   length of time. There are 24 hours in a day.

leap second   extra second that is added from time to time to keep our clocks in step with the gradually slowing Earth

leap year   year with 366 days

minute   length of time. There are 60 minutes in an hour.

month   length of time based on the time it takes for the Moon to orbit Earth once

nighttime   time between sunset and sunrise

Northern Hemisphere   half of Earth north of the equator; the top half of a globe

observatory   building where astronomers make observations with telescopes and other instruments

orbit   path of a planet around the Sun, or of a moon around a planet

pendulum   swinging wooden or metal rod (or length of thread) with a weight attached to its lower end

quartz   crystalline mineral. A quartz timer is used in most modern clocks and watches.

satellite   object that orbits Earth or another planet. Some satellites send back information to scientists.

second   length of time. There are 60 seconds in a minute.

Southern Hemisphere   half of Earth south of the equator; the bottom half of a globe

sundial   device that uses shadows to find the time from the Sun's position in the sky

telescope   instrument that makes distant objects appear both nearer and larger

timer   device used for measuring a specific interval of time

vibrate   to move rapidly back and forth

watch   small timekeeper that has been designed to be carried around or worn

week   length of time. There are seven days in a week.

year   length of time based on the time taken for Earth to orbit the Sun once and for the cycle of seasons to repeat itself. A normal calendar year has 365 days. A leap year has 366 days.

More Books to Read

Shapiro, Irwin I. and Marvin C. Grossman. *ARIES Exploring Time: Sundials, Water Clocks, & Pendulums: Science Journal.* Watertown, Mass.: Charlesbridge Publishers, Inc., 2000.

Snedden, Robert. *Time.* Broomall, Pa.: Chelsea House Publishers, 1995.

Walpole, Brenda. *Time.* Milwaukee, Wis.: Gareth Stevens Inc., 1995.

Index